Elegy with Clouds &

Elegy with Clouds &

poems

Robin Turner

.

Cover design by Shay Culligan
Cover art by Chris F on Pexels

ISBN: 978-1-63980-721-5

Kelsay Books
502 South 1040 East, A-119
American Fork, Utah 84003
Kelsaybooks.com

for my mother
for all our mothers
in memory

&

for my family
nest & knot & always

Acknowledgments

Grateful acknowledgment is made to the following publications where these poems first appeared, sometimes with a different title or in a slightly altered form.

Anima Poetry: "Night Ocean"
Autumn Sky Poetry Daily: "When My Mother Forgets the Word for Dahlia"
Cider Press Review: "Here & Here & Here"
DMQ Review: "Suspended"
Dream Geographies: "The Days"
Ethel: "Water"
Four & Twenty: "There Now"
The Fourth River—Tributaries: "Presence"
Journal of Compressed Creative Arts: "Come Back"
MacQueen's Quinterly: "Elegy with Clouds & Breakfast Cereal," "Flight"
Pithead Chapel: "In a World All But Buried"
Rattle Magazine: "Little Bird"
Red River Review: "To Make This Love Poem"
Referential Magazine: "For the Swan at White Rock"
River Mouth Review: "The Doorway"
Sweet Lit: "After the Swailing at Little Pine Lake," "All This Way"
Thin Spaces & Sacred Places (anthology, Amethyst Review Press): "Near the End of the Sorrow Season"

Contents

III

Somewhere the Child

a cento

The wind wraps all of us with winter.
Ghosts & demons & fierce flaming angels.

That shift of light, arpeggio.
Somewhere the child I was is wailing.

When the mothers leave,
what are we supposed to do?

I

To Make This Love Poem

I draw down some stars
dipped in night sky blue.

I bleed a little,
bleed a lot,

let my page of stars catch
each droplet.

Now to fold—*no*—
crumple the paper.

Form it into a ball
that resembles a world.

Where blood meets blue
a poem blooms.

That field of strange flowers.
Wild riot of violet & fierce purple.

You have to flatten the paper
to see it—this love poem

of beautiful bruise.

When My Mother Forgets the Word for Dahlia

Picking a favorite dahlia is like going through a button box.
—The Old Farmers Almanac

When my mother forgets the word for dahlia
it is February. It is the last day of her 84th year, the latest day
in a ruthless unspooling of days, of pandemic lockdown,
its cruel isolation, & winter, all the gardens covered over,
all our lives fallow, fallow. When my mother forgets

the word for *dahlia,* tall flower as familiar to her as a daughter,
its name soft as psalm on the tongue, it is yet another day
of all the distances between us—every long year apart,
every rocky geography, every hurt forgiven & not
forgiven. And in that instant every distance opens wide

its spacious arms as every distance collapses & gathers
as *dahlia* waits snug in its button box to be found, tucked
just out of memory's reach until it passes like miracle into me,
blossoming into speech—*dahlia* I say through the phone & into
my mother's frustrated silence, her solitary sorting, sorting.

I give her back the beloved, the favorite flower, the one
she knows but can no longer name. When my mother forgets
the word for *dahlia,* I drive in a blinding rain to the wizened
women at the nursery called Blue Moon. They will know.
They will know the flower I have come for.

The Rain Has Stopped

A tornado watch appears
on my phone low-glowing.

My sister calls, all cigarettes
& grit, to tell me another day

of the news—
our mother's long slow-going

from this world, her wounds
& her woundedness turned up

bright this night. Outside
a full winter moon blazes

just above the bare bones
of the treetops, the night sky

an impossible bruise.
Clouds ghost past, a river

of gauze that won't quit
& won't stick.

Night Ocean

Alone in the world's wide doorway,
a small girl in red sneakers. Silent.

She holds the night ocean high above her.
Impossible weighted water, great

rectangle of stubborn glass.
If I move to lift it from her, all is lost.

Between us the space is quiet.
Between us all is white—

not the weather-worn white of stone or seashell
but the color of stillness just before.

Her strength settles in me like heartbeat.
I do not dream her again.

Water

Make of me an emptiness,
a morning clear & present,

night's terrors muted,
its details obscure.

Carve me. Crush me. Shadow-
shift me. Make me

a figure shining.

For the Swan at White Rock

I visit you at sunset
for weeks on end, memorize

your slender neck, each movement,
slow white grace on our mud-thick lake.

Bright apparition
from the root of dusk,

you have seamed yourself
to the liquid lining of my vision,

dreamed your body into mine.
There in the space between sleep

and waking you float—a wild thing
mute

and unburdened.
Some have seen you fly.

I practice silence,
grow impractical white feathers.

I study the strength of white wings.

Presence

What falls away is always. And is near.
　　　　　　—Theodore Roethke

They have been over & around us, above
& below us, reflected on water, all weather

& wonder, steadfast & absent, a storm.
They have been name-that-shape as we gaze

from the grassy banks, chariot for saints
& for sinners, soft cotton batting, friend,

apparition. Today they are the stuff of my mother's
late dreaming. They flood the snug room

where she sleeps. *God calling,* she tells me
from this side of slow waking. Heaven

trying her on for size. She pushes Heaven away
with her hands, swats at God as she would a pest buzzing.

We drink tea honey-sweet, steep ourselves deep in the Here
& the Now. Mother's clouds Holy Ghost it to the next town over.

I watch them gather, reconfigure
in the near distant sky.

Even in Winter

Mother
could not abide

a shut door a closed room
wanted her bedside window open

      to sky
                any sky

Blue on Blue

after Ruth Stone

Larkspur, delphinium, blue
morning glory. Bluebonnets,

bluets, cornflower blue.
Blue pink gill, blue milk cap,

blue baby booties. Pulsing blue
veins through the skin of our wrists.

Blue eyes, lapis lazuli, the blue nudes
of Matisse. True blue, out of the blue,

blue ink on blue paper. Blue willow china,
blue lips in blue light.

Now

The mornings keep tracing
leaf shadow & light on the living.
All the small, beautiful things.

My mother doesn't see them
now. My mother doesn't.
Isn't.

My mother.
My mother.
My mother.

Here & Here & Here

after Rose-Lynn Fisher's "after goodbye"

like stitches
like scratches

like scars on the skin
like crossroads littered

like pavement cracked
like X marks the spot   here

   & here

        & here—
    a gash in the surface of the moon

II

Through the Shallows

Fish glint in a wide puddle
the rain has left, ghosts darting

through the shallows. All day
I will wonder how they got here

& this—
How will they ever get home?

Keen

—a lamentation for the dead

In the hours just after, ~~someone~~
said *About the obituary, do me a favor.*
~~Someone~~ said *Don't use*
her maiden name. Leave it out.

~~Someone~~ said *the dark web.*
~~Someone's~~ *high profile business executive*
status. Identity theft. Identity theft.
Identity theft ~~someone~~ said & said & said.

200 words is all we need. All ~~someone's~~
friends-in-the-know had said so.
I said *86 years of living.* I said
our ancestors. I said *Keene.*

Keene Keene Keene Keene
Keene Keene Keene times two,
times ten, times twenty. I said
her name. I say it & say it & say.

I count. I wail. I ad infinitum.
Keene Keene Keene Keene. I sing
my mother out of this world.
I sing my mother back.

About the Theft—

I can never retrieve
those hours. Holy hours. *Stolen.*
Stolen. Stolen.

In a World All But Buried

in tin cans & cellophane, in cigarette butts & chewing gum, in Big Gulp cups after the big gulp, forgive me. Forgive me for mistaking a wadded tissue tossed into leaf litter for a perfect puff of cloud fallen from the sky. It floated me all the way home.

Flight

Waiting for my flight after
burying our mother, I cry. I cry
when I realize I've left behind
a small gift for a friend. Each
lesser loss now a great piercing. I cry
as I order sunflowers for my sister.
Nearby in the terminal another woman
weeps, her own mother disappearing
into the security line abyss, returning
to the old country, to a home far from here,
each tearing an agony. I flee
to the restroom, wash my face, swallow hard,
gather myself before boarding begins.
On the plane, flanked by families,
their babies take up crying, inconsolable.
The smallest, an infant, is a purist. Her wailing
a three-hour raw lamentation, all vowel
& howl, eternal. The older baby knows *No!*
& screams it—repeating crescendos
of *No Nooo Noooooooo.* We hurtle
through the heavens, tethered
& untethered, outside civilization,
unthinking, animals keening
through this longest night.

Suspended

Oh, we say it all the time—*It's a jungle out there.* Meaning, the world, the mean streets, the workaday weeks, their dense tangle. You grip your car's steering wheel, which is to say—your life. You focus, try not to think of the dream of the overpass, the car flying straight off its edge & out into air. And every time the surprise—of waking, wondering, suspended, not knowing. Have you fallen. Have you flown.

Little Bird

for Artie

The hottest month of the hottest year
on record. August in Texas. Unrelenting.

Mother had died just the month before.
My mother. The world kept burning.

And on the news, on our phones, all week the photos
of treasonous men, their arrogant mugshots

marring every screen, suffocating each sensible citizen.
How to breathe through the heat, through the spin

& the grief? How to rescue from harm what one loves?
When a red-feathered bird crashed into our window, it fell

like a stone & lay motionless. *Little bird,* you said
& stepped out to the porch, bent to stroke, to *tap tap* her still chest,

brought ice, brought tenderness, prayed mercy.
In the morning you spared me

from shoveling parched earth
& gave up the lost creature to ground.

You knew, knew I would not be able to bury her—
one more once beautiful thing.

After the Swailing at Little Pine Lake

For days wisps of smoke slow ghost it all along the still water's ember edge. I watch them shapeshift from the safety of my rented cabin just up the hill. Sleep & dream. Sleep & dream. Make notes. What lingers. What haunts. What rises & goes. After the burning.

Near the End of the Sorrow Season

the carpenter comes,
removes the stubborn old door

that had darkened our living room for days
& sets to work installing a new one

made to order. He is thoughtful
as he labors, meticulous

as a surgeon or a builder of nests,
a holy man with toolbelt & kind eyes.

He finishes the job & we stand & praise
as the door pours forth its benediction of light.

The door has four perfect windows.
Its hinges give & gleam.

III

The Doorway

a cento

Willows & the river,
the dark red tulip,
stone & tree & sky.
The birds know a day.
At times you spoke, at other times you were silent,
& in languages that aren't always sound.
All the failed echoes,
a word of praise,
before letting each fragment drop.
At the doorway, I watched, & I suddenly—
I just walked through them.

Elegy with Clouds & Breakfast Cereal

Red River, New Mexico

Even in places she had never been, my mother
now is, once was, will be. An absence &

an everywhere, a before & an after, my trickster
mother, a shape ever shifting. Three months dead

& she comes up with the sun over the ridge,
scattering into scraps of cloud

petal pink. They float along light
like those little circles of cereal sweet

in my childhood's breakfast bowl.
Mother nearby at a sink full of soap suds

or packing the lunch boxes for school.
I would spoon every soggy bit

into my mouth, wipe my chin, then drink
all the sugared milk down.

The Days

There will be days. A sea-green peace holds us
where water meets the sky. Monet's lily pond
lives in us, breathes in us, untroubled,
dreaming slow. Sister Libertas, steadfast
in her soft veil of fog, lifts high the light eternal,
stays near to us as spirit. We are free.
We are floating, tender as children just out of school,
our little pipe-cleaner amulets, our skinny legs,
painted paddleboards. All is buoyant. All is right.
There will be other days. Be ready. The heavy wings
of a sudden darkness may come for you. Feed it
only what little you can spare, a raw lily, the smallest
offering, nothing more. Feel its swift pierce, its quick
turning. Feel it leave you. Watch it go. Return
to your breath, your birthright, the still waters, your body
a bright garden, sacred harbor, gleaming teal.

There Now

Soft rain
of catkins
hushes
the noise
in my
too full head.
Gentles the day
like a good mother.

Postcard from White Rock

Woolen clouds crowd
a wide sky, generous,

mother soft. They cover us,
tuck us in to sleep & dream.

Make a wish comes the whisper.
The winter trees have all

but bared themselves. They reach
& reach their long limbs

toward your voice.
Wish you were here.

Come Back

It's spring & I'm thinking of the things that come back—macrame & low-rise blue jeans, the scissor-tails & the ruby throats, wild primrose & thistle & thyme. I have seen them. Old gospel songs & Polaroids, the first & the last days of school, &—so they tell us— Jesus. I am waiting for the coming of some late summer rain, the return of the red resurrection flower, its strong-tender stem, its intricate blossom a year's dark, deepening. I am waiting for my mother.

Walking at White Rock

held in blue air—

The sky is my mother.
The sky is my mother.
The sky is my mother now.

How Far

Now heat bakes the fields. Wrings us
turns us inside out. Hollow

bottles rattle, half-wild, forsaken.
Every weed-dusted window

a photograph framed. Ghosts & crows.
Time outlined & praying. Tell me—

Which pretty pictures to pin to the sky?
How far from spring have we come?

All This Way

My mother, alive again, speaking to me—what *was* it?—from a small space near a window. A cramped space. An unfamiliar room. And the light there. Dull. Dim. Unremarkable. Light not lighting, not gathering, around my mother. Had I summoned her? This dreary space. She'd come all this way. Through this porous universe. Slipped in between two slats of bent blinds covered with dust. Slipped back into this bent & broken world. To tell me something. To tell me. To tell.

Notes

"Somewhere the Child" is a cento composed of lines from Sheila Packa, Marge Piercy, Denise Levertov, Judith E. Prest, and Victoria Chang. The word "and" has been replaced with ampersands.

"Blue on Blue" is after Ruth Stone's "White on White."

"Here & Here & Here" is an ekphrastic inspired by Rose-Lynn Fisher's "after goodbye" from her book of microphotographs, *The Topography of Tears.*

"After the Swailing at Little Pine Lake": The word "swailing" is an old term for prescribed burning, the art of managing and clearing the ground of dead vegetation so that new growth can occur.

"The Doorway" is a cento composed of lines from *A God in the House: poets talk about faith,* edited by Ilya Kaminsky and Katherine Towler. Lines are from Gregory Orr, Alicia Ostriker, Christian Wiman, Jericho Brown, Jane Hirshfield, Joy Harjo, Kazim Ali, Dunya Mikhail, G.C. Waldrop, Li-Young Lee, and Marilyn Nelson. The word "and" has been replaced with ampersands.

About the Poet

Robin Turner's poems, prose poems, and flash fiction appear in numerous publications, among them *Rattle, The Texas Observer, Rust + Moth, DMQ Review, One,* and *Bracken Magazine.* Her work has been tucked inside little poetry houses in Pittsburgh, paired with photographs in a Deep Ellum art gallery, transformed into tiny artist books for the White Rock Zine Machine, and collected in a handbound micro chapbook: *bindweed & crow poison* (Porkbelly Press). A longtime community teaching artist and sometime reader for *Sugared Water,* she lives near White Rock Lake in Dallas, Texas.

Made in the USA
Columbia, SC
20 March 2025

55441334R00036